Present Day
Miracles
at
Teen Challenge

4 stories of deliverance from drug addiction

David Batty

D1316180

Third Edition 2016

Cover design by Doug Raught and Don Jones

ISBN: 978-1533144232

Printed in the United States of America.

To order additional copies, contact:

David Batty
3215 Thornberry Circle
Phenix City, AL 36867
Phone: 706-536-5813
Email: DBatty@gmail.com

For a listing of Teen Challenge centers

USA listing: www.TeenChallengeUSA.com
Phone: 417-581-2181

International listing: www.GlobalTC.org
Phone: 706-576-6555

Contents

Introduction

Every young man and woman who graduates from Teen Challenge is truly a modern-day miracle. As I look at the thousands who have come through the doors of Teen Challenge in Brooklyn, New York and other centers across the nation and around the world, I can only say—to God be the glory, great things He has done!

They come bound by addiction, carrying deep damage from a lifestyle that smashed every one of their dreams and hopes for life. The damage is far greater than drug addiction—it has impacted every area of their lives and family relationships.

When I listen to their stories, I'm amazed they are even alive today—the miracles began long before they entered Teen Challenge. Most were unaware that God's hand was on them, patiently leading them to a place where they could experience His transforming miracles.

For many who come, the miracles do not always occur in a dramatic instant. The process takes months for some, such as Elizabeth. "It was 7 months before I began to believe that I could be a normal person," she stated. She began her path to addiction as an 8 year old in a family of alcoholics.

Sonny explained, "It was 10 years after graduating from Teen Challenge before he woke up in the morning no longer thinking like a drug addict. Now when I think back to those years when I was an addict, it's like it wasn't even me."

Others like Johnny Melendez, whose story you will read in this book, experienced a dramatic conversion and healing the first day at Teen Challenge. As a result of those miracles, he never experienced withdrawal pains from the drugs he was addicted to for so many years.

The four stories that follow are only a tiny sample of the incredible miracles we have seen at Teen Challenge. All the miracles in each broken life are the work of Jesus Christ. Often God has used the dedicated staff to be a key part of these miracles.

Each story is written in the first person, in the words of Johnny Melendez, Canzada Edmonds, and Paul Patrick. The exception is Ralph Rodriguez whose story is told through the accounts of the staff and students who knew and loved him deeply.

The year listed in the title of each chapter tells when that person came to Teen Challenge and began to experience God's miracle of transformation. I want you to know these changes last for a lifetime! There are many other more recent testimonies of those who have experienced the same change.

I hope you gain new insights on how to best help your loved ones who may be caught up in an addiction or other life-controlling problems.

Since 1958, this ministry has been the setting for thousands of miracles. The miracles are not done yet! There are drug addicts on the streets of New York City and around the world today who are lost in despair and hopelessness. They see no way out of their desperate situation. But God has a plan for their future, filled with hope. They don't know it yet, but in the months ahead God is going to bring them to Teen Challenge where they will experience a miracle just as great as the ones told in this book.

You can be part of these new miracles as you share this message of hope with a friend or stranger caught in addiction.

The most important way you can be part of a new miracle is to join us in praying for that miracle to occur in the life of each new student coming into Teen Challenge today.

Page 93 gives a brief explanation of how someone can receive help at Teen Challenge. On page 92, is a description of how you can experience a miracle in your life today.

Dave Batty
Email: DBatty@gmail.com

From the Dragons gang
to Lieutenant Colonel, U.S. Army

Johnny Melendez 1964

When I came through the door of Teen Challenge at 416 Clinton Ave., in Brooklyn, New York, on that cold night in February 1964, I came with a lot of confusion. I was a broken, hurting, addicted young man unable to see beyond the chaos of my life.

If you had told me what God would do in my life over the next 40 years, I would have responded that you were crazy and needed to be locked up in a psych ward!

I came from Puerto Rico to live in New York City when I was 5 years old. In Spanish Harlem, I grew up around drugs, with guys shooting up on the rooftop of my building, smoking pot in the hallways.

These early years of my life I lived with no hope and no future. I dropped out of school in the 7th grade.

By the time I was a teenager, I got involved in a gang—the Dragons. This was the largest gang in New York City, and it was born right on my block on 107th Street in the Bronx. In order to survive on the streets, I had to belong to something, so I joined that gang.

One day I was with a couple of friends and young ladies who were part of the gang, listening to doo-wop music. There was a knock on the door, and this guy Sammy said, "Little Willie wants to see you downstairs." I said, OK. I knew Little Willie, he was a member of the Viceroy gang. I wasn't afraid of him—but I didn't know he had a gun.

As we came down the stairs, he took me to the back of the stairs with my friend Pete, who was the president of the Seminal Dragons which was a brother gang. Pete was my best friend who later died in a shootout. Little Willie pulled out a gun which was a 45, and he pulled the trigger back and put it on my forehead. Then he asked Sammy in a cocky way, "Should we burn him now? Should we burn him?"

At that very moment some people came into the building, so Little Willie put his gun away. And then they had to get out of our territory for there were Dragons out there. They made us leave the building walking right in front of them, and they said, "If you make a move we are going to shoot you on the spot."

As Pete and I were walking down the sidewalk, and Little Willie and Sammy were right behind us, the other guys from my gang had no idea what was going on. They thought we were talking about some other things related to the gang.

Little Willie and Sammy jumped in a car that was waiting for them and went back to their territory.

I went back to our armory down in the basement of our building and took out a 45, and put a clip in it, and put it under my shirt. Pete and I went down in the Viceroy territory to look for Little Willie. Our plan was to shoot him in the doorway of his home. We went to the apartment building where he lived, and we knocked on the door, but it was the wrong one. We knocked on another door, and it was not that one, and we kept on knocking on doors. Finally we gave up and left.

My mother found out about it—I was her only son— and she sent me to Puerto Rico for a while, hoping this would help get me straightened out. While I was there I joined the National Guard, even though I was too young. My uncle helped me lie about my age so I could get in.

A couple years later I came back to New York. When I came back I got into drugs—for the next 7 years I was lost in the streets of Spanish Harlem and New York City.

I didn't want to see my mother suffer any more, so I stopped living at home. I started living in a basement on 119th Street in Manhattan. I used to flatten out the coal that was there, and put cardboard on top—that was my bed, close to the furnace so I could stay warm in the winter.

The building superintendent would let me stay down there because I would help him keep the building clean, and I would shovel the coal into the boiler. Looking back now I can see I was practicing for hell.

I remember praying in that basement, "God, if there is a God, please help me."

One day I stood there in that basement, all alone, looking into that fire inside the boiler, trying to stay warm. It was almost Christmas, and I didn't want to go back out into the cold night, because in my head I was hearing my Mom saying, "You're going to get killed. You're going to die of an overdose."

I had already overdosed twice, once when I was alone. Once I saved my buddy's life. I said to myself, "I've got to get out of this life."

One of my friends invited me to go to a séance—at first I resisted. My grandmother was a devout Catholic and she had instilled in me the basic teachings about God. Even though I never had a relationship with God, I knew that this séance was different. But my friend finally talked me into going. At this séance there was a whole row of people, a table in the middle, and people dressed in white. There they called in the spirits, and some kind of spirit came—got into this lady, and she began to walk around like a chicken.

She asked for a big cigar, and she began to walk down the aisle, all the way to the back where I was, and she grabbed me, and she pulled me up. I didn't want to go, but my buddy, next to me said, "Go ahead." So I went with her to the middle of the table, there she stood before me and blew smoke all over me.

She took out a piece of paper, a pencil, and looked deep into my eyes. Then she began to write real fast. She gave me the paper and pointed me to go to another room to interpret it. One of the things she said, "You have a short time to live. If you don't listen to this good spirit that is trying to reach you, the spirit will leave you to your own destruction."

I was very worried that night after the séance. I told my mom, "I've got to kick this dirty habit. I'm going to stay home this time until I kick this addiction." So she agreed to help me. I got in bed, and you know how it goes, the pains, the joints, the fever, the hot and cold. My mom came over to the bed and put Vicks over my whole body.

The pain got so bad that I couldn't take it any more. This was no different than all the other times I had tried to kick drugs. So I got up about 3 o'clock in the morning, and told my mom, "I can't stay here."

When I went out I saw a friend of mine, Mo. He was

sitting in a bakery shop, reading a little card. So I asked him, "What are you reading?" He said, "It's a card this guy from Teen Challenge gave me, and he told me if I wanted to kick my drug habit to come down to Teen Challenge." Mo didn't want the card, so he gave it to me.

I took the card home, and about 10 o'clock in the morning I was talking to my mom. She was crying as she said, "You are going kill yourself. Somebody's going to call me and say you've been shot."

Just to pacify her, I took the card out of my pocket and said, "Look Mom, I'm trying." She looked at the card and said, "Why don't you call this place? Maybe they have new doctors. Maybe they have a new cure, or new medicines."

I told her, "OK, I'll call."

So I called the number and Nicky Cruz answered the phone. I said, "I'm John Melendez, and I really need some help." He said to me, "Johnny, if you really want some help,

I want you to wait for me on 125th Street. We are going to have a street meeting there tonight."

I went there that night in February—it was so cold I was shaking. Nicky gave me his coat and put me into the Teen Challenge van. Crazy things were happening inside the van—these people were hitting the side of the van and singing, "there is power in the blood."

That night, when I went down to Teen Challenge at 416 Clinton Ave., in Brooklyn, Nicky pulled me into his office with his friend, Fedorico. He put a gray chair in the middle, and said, "Sit down, Johnny, we are going to pray for you."

"Nicky," I said, "I'm Catholic, and you are not going to change my religion." Nicky started praying, in a way that I was not used to praying—loud and intense. Then he stopped. "Johnny, if you want God to help you, then you have to ask God yourself." So he grabbed one of my arms and held it up in the air. When Federico saw that, he grabbed my other arm and put it up in the air. Then they started praying again.

Pretty soon they didn't have to hold up my hands any more. I began to pray really hard, from way down deep inside. I began to cry out to God, "Please God, help me! Make me a new man! Change my life!" At that point Jesus came into my life, and He began to make me into a new person.

The next day Nicky came over to my bedside and he said, "Something must have happened last night." Another guy came over, hugged me and said, "The Lord healed you last night. You know that—right?" I didn't really understand the word "healing" at that time, but I said, "I guess so."

For the next few days I kept waiting for the withdrawal pains to start, but they never came. That night Jesus Christ came into my life, He truly did heal me, because I never went through any withdrawal pains from the drugs I had been using.

In just two or three weeks, they took me to the Teen Challenge farm in Rehrersburg, Pennsylvania, where I could continue my growth. We had classes every day, and chapel services every day. I remember the staff praying for me. They would find me in the chapel alone, they would come and kneel down and put their hands on me and pray for me.

We memorized a lot a scriptures in our classes, and 2 Corinthians 5:17 was one that gave me hope for a new future. "Therefore, if anyone is in Christ, he is a new creation; the old has gone, the new has come!" I knew I had a lot of growth that needed to take place, but now I had the hope that God would radically change me.

I made a plaque and put it on top of the window in my room. It said, "My grace is sufficient for you," from 2 Corinthians 12:9 where God goes on to say, "My power is made perfect in weakness." That gave me such hope. I had been such a failure, a 7th grade drop out. But now God was giving me a love for studying His word.

Kathryn Kuhlman, the nationally known evangelist,

came and spoke in chapel. She would go to each one of the students and pray for us, and God would touch us in a very special way.

When I graduated from Teen Challenge, I came back to Brooklyn and worked as a staff member at the men's program. Soon I was teaching the Bible classes to the new students coming into Brooklyn. On weekends I would go out to churches and share my testimony.

I worked with Mom Wilkerson in the coffeehouse in Greenwich Village. That was the first time I witnessed to people outside the church.

We would also take a group of staff and students up to Spanish Harlem and preach on the streets, much like Nicky Cruz did the night I came into Teen Challenge. There would be times when young boys up on the rooftops would throw food down on me as I was preaching. That really didn't surprise me, because when I was a young teenager, I used to do the same thing when people would be preaching on the streets.

I went to Bible college in Pennsylvania—what a struggle that was for a 7th grade drop out! But God helped me. I had to drop out after 2 years because I could not pay my school bills. I came back to Brooklyn, worked at Teen Challenge and also got a second job working at a grocery store. For the first time in my life I paid off a debt, so I could return to college.

God opened another door to attend Southwestern Bible College in Waxahachie, Texas, where I earned a Bachelor of Science degree. After graduating I got married and went to work at the Teen Challenge Institute of Missions in Rhinebeck, New York, a school for graduates of Teen Challenge who wanted to prepare for the ministry.

Two years later I entered Fuller Theological Seminary in Pasadena, California, and completed a Masters of Divinity degree. After graduating in 1976, God opened the door for me to be accepted into the U.S. Army as a military chaplain.

I served three tours in Germany, then on to Saudi Arabia, Iraq and Kuwait during Desert Shield and Desert Storm, Albania, Macedonia, and Kosovo. I retired with the rank of Lieutenant Colonel on April 30, 2002, with 26 years of service as a U.S. Army Chaplain.

When I look back at those years of ministry, when I preached to privates all the way up to generals, I am simply amazed at what God can do with a Teen Challenge graduate!

Graduation day with AIDS and Honors

Ralph Rodriguez 1984

Graduation day, his first ever! "One of the best days of my life!" Ralph testified. The fact that he was barely able to read did not diminish the joy he experienced on this special day. Now 31 years old, he was graduating from Teen Challenge.

Feelings of sadness, hope, and anticipation also churned inside Ralph. Sadness because his girlfriend was not present. He shared the same prayer request again, "Please pray for my girlfriend that she will leave her life of drug addiction and give her life to Christ."

Hope and anticipation also pumped in Ralph's heart as he looked at his first real job opportunity in years. For over 15 years he had made his living through crime—scheming, conning, robbing anyone to get money for his drugs.

God's transforming work had brought radical change to Ralph's life. He had entered Teen Challenge one year earlier a street hardened, selfish, sullen, broken man. Years of drug addiction, street crime and prison had taken their toll on him.

The day he came to Teen Challenge had started badly. Ralph was in a shooting gallery—an old abandoned building in Spanish Harlem used by drug addicts as a place to meet and get high. He was already sick because it had been too long since his last shot of heroin.

Finally with a new bag of dope in his hands, he hurried to shoot the drugs into his veins—but it was fake dope—it wasn't real heroin. After he shot it up, he only became sicker.

Plunging into even deeper despair, he looked up on the dirty walls of the shooting gallery and his eyes fell on a graffiti message spray painted on the wall. "Jesus loves you." And below that, "If you need help call" and a phone number was listed.

Ralph stumbled out of the building and called that number. Cosmos, a Teen Challenge graduate, answered the phone and assured Ralph that indeed there was help for him at a program called Teen Challenge. Cosmos rushed to the building and brought Ralph straight to Teen Challenge in Brooklyn.

The first days at Teen Challenge were not easy. Even though he was desperate to change, Ralph was filled with anger, despair, and confusion. Other students described him as the meanest con artist in Teen Challenge.

In those early days at Teen Challenge Ralph seemed to have a breakthrough in his life. But the pull of drugs and his girlfriend were too much. In a few weeks he left and returned to his lifestyle of crime and drugs.

He soon ended up in jail again, where he had plenty of time to think about all the chapel services and Bible classes he had attended at Teen Challenge. One of the art teachers in the jail noticed Ralph's talent and challenged him, "When you get out of jail, come and see me, and I will get you a scholarship into an art school in New York City."

As soon as his sentence was up, Ralph returned to Teen Challenge, but this time he came determined to change. With his limited reading skills, he really struggled with the assignments for his daily Bible classes. When he started memorizing Bible verses, he began to see a real improvement in his reading.

After one year in the program, Ralph had earned a new reputation as a loving, caring man with a genuine passion to share God's love with others.

On the day Ralph graduated from Teen Challenge, he shared his hopes for the future. "I have three goals. First, I want to tell others about Jesus and share with them the freedom Christ brought to my life," he stated with a passion from deep within.

"Second, I want to see my girlfriend experience deliverance from her addiction.

"Third, I want to attend art school." He still wanted to follow up on that offer of a full scholarship.

Immediately after graduating, he came on staff at Teen Challenge in Brooklyn. As the night watchman, he always encouraged the new students to serve Jesus 100% and not turn back to drugs. His genuine love for others and his compassion was so encouraging to the new students who were struggling with the same issues he had faced in his first days at Teen Challenge.

When the phone rang late at night, he would eagerly share his testimony of how God had set him free from over 15 years of drug addiction and radically changed his life.

One night he was in his bedroom and heard screams as a young man snatched the purse from Phyllis Davis, one of the new staff at Teen Challenge. Ralph raced down the stairs and out the front door, and caught up with the thief, grabbed him and wanted to punch him out. Instead, he threw the man to the ground, and said, "Jesus loves you, now get your life right!" The startled thief offered no resistance as Ralph took the stolen purse and returned it to Phyllis.

As Ralph rode the bus to art school in Brooklyn, he

would look for people with despair written on their faces and share with them the hope that had transformed his life.

On weekends Ralph would go to surrounding churches with the Teen Challenge students and share his testimony of deliverance. God gifted him with a beautiful voice, and Ralph loved to sing Christian songs, expressing his love to God.

One day he went back to his old neighborhood in Brooklyn looking for opportunities to share Jesus with others. He saw one of his old drug buddies, and called out his name. The man just ignored him, so Ralph called out his name again. "Who are you?" snarled the man.

"I'm Ralph!"

The guy replied, "I don't know you."

Then Ralph told him his street name—the man just stared at him in disbelief. "What did you do? Did you have plastic surgery?"

Ralph responded, "No! This is Jesus! Jesus changed me!" And he launched into his testimony with great enthusiasm.

One of Ralph's greatest joys was the day he was able to see his mother give her heart to Jesus, and experience the same salvation that had radically transformed his life.

The art school had never seen a student like Ralph. His life of drugs and crime had aged him prematurely. His contagious smile was distinctive with several teeth missing. Every art assignment he completed included a scripture verse–unheard of in this secular art school setting.

Over the next two years Ralph continued to show a deep, unconditional love to his girlfriend. He helped her get into Teen Challenge, but after a few weeks she left. Several more programs led to the same premature dropout. But he kept praying.

Then came the biggest test in his life, the discovery that he had AIDS.

This did not deter his fervor to witness; instead he turned this into a new opportunity to witness to others. His joyful smile was an encouragement to friends who visited him in the hospital.

Nurses and doctors could not understand why he was acting this way. He was only too glad to tell them how Jesus had transformed his life.

When he became too ill to get out of bed to talk to the other patients, the nurses would bring them into his room so he could share with them the secret to his joy.

One Sunday morning in June 1987, a call came to Teen Challenge from the hospital to announce Ralph's death. His final graduation day surely eclipsed his graduation from Teen Challenge and art school. Surely it was an awesome experience in heaven on that Sunday morning when he heard his heavenly Father say, "Well done, Ralph, you've been a good and faithful servant."

When the Teen Challenge staff visited his mother later that day, she had one final request. "My son was dead for so many years, and Teen Challenge gave him back to me alive. Will you allow my son's funeral to be at Teen Challenge?"

Later that week 400 people gathered from all walks of life, impacted by Ralph's deep love and compassion. The hall into the chapel was lined with his art work. A graduate of Teen Challenge shared how Ralph had been the one to encourage him to stay in the program. Even in death, Ralph's testimony was still impacting people.

Sketch by Ralph based on Psalm 42:2-3,

2. My soul thirsts for God, for the living God.

When can I go and meet with God?

3. My tears have been my food day and night.

Every piece of art Ralph Rodriguez created for the secular art school he attended included a scripture—his way of communicating to others the dramatic change Christ had brought into his life after 15 years of drug addiction.

You've heard, "They have to hit bottom
before they will get help."

Why not
"Raise the bottom!"

You've heard it said, "They must hit bottom before
they will be ready to get help." Do you have to wait until
they hit bottom? Or is there something you can do to help
"raise the bottom" so your loved one can get help sooner?

What does it mean to "hit bottom?"

We often look at a person who has lost everything—
job, car, home, respect. Often family relationships have been
destroyed by broken promises. They "hit bottom" when they
are homeless and living on the streets. They've hit bottom
when no one will loan them money to make it through their
current "crisis."

One ex-addict told me, " 'Hitting bottom' meant giving
up my dignity and self-respect—doing whatever it took to get
money for drugs. I even sold my body for a few dollars."

For another young mother on her way to "hitting
bottom" it meant losing custody of her children—and still
falling deeper into her addiction.

" 'Hitting bottom' meant I was in so much pain—I was sick and tired of being sick and tired. 'Hitting bottom' meant I was ready to change—to give up on my miserable life and find help."

"Hitting bottom" means facing reality—hitting a hard painful place—with nowhere else to go.

For some, it means being penniless—hungry—even starving. The pain can no longer be ignored or drowned out with drugs or alcohol.

"When I finally came to the end of myself and said, 'I need help.' That was the beginning of my road to recovery," shares one young man. "I was finally ready to listen to others."

"Hitting bottom" means a person is forced to face the consequences of their irresponsible lifestyle—it is not easy— many are very stubborn.

"I had been going blindly down the road to destruction—but convinced it was the best way to go," explained another young man.

"I had given up on life—I was so miserable, I wanted to die. 'Hitting bottom' meant I could no longer run from reality. Denial and delusion had taken me down a dead-end street."

The common trait of those who "hit bottom"

What is the common trait of those who "hit bottom," and survive? Pain!

"I was in so much pain, I wanted to die," shared one young lady here at Teen Challenge. "The pain helped me face reality—the pain was real—I couldn't run from it or deny it any longer."

For those who have "hit bottom" and recovered, that path to restoration is often slow and painful.

"I had to be willing to face my problems—and I had lots of them," Elisa shared. "When I called my mother from a pay phone, she came and got me off the street and helped me get into Teen Challenge where I found God's answers to my problems.

"When I first came to Teen Challenge, I was so confused. I rebelled against the staff. I was moody and inconsistent— up one day and down the next. But the staff persisted in showing me love, and holding me responsible for

> **For many years I could not identify with hitting bottom,** because I was living a life of deception. I was blind to hitting bottom. I could not identify with the concept—even when I lost jobs. I hit bottom on October 8, 1992, when I tried to commit suicide.
> —*Canzada Edmonds*

my actions. Slowly the fog cleared from my mind.

"It's been a painful process—but I am finally getting myself on a solid foundation where I can move toward healthy relationships. I'm learning what it means to take responsibility for my actions, my words, and my feelings.

"I could not have made these changes on my own. It took God's love and God's power to change me. When I surrendered my will to Him, that's when the real changes on the inside started."

"Hitting bottom" became the turning point for many— but not for all. Some hit bottom and commit suicide. Others end up in prison for life.

So what about your loved one—on the road to destruction—using drugs or alcohol or some other destructive behavior? They

---

My boyfriend supported my drug habit for over 10 years. And then he ended up in jail. Always before I could get a friend to give me money. But now my friends told me to stay away. They didn't trust me any more.

I had lied to them so many times, they didn't want to have anything to do with me. I had lost custody of my children. When no one would help me, I finally began to believe that I needed to get help.

may be hurting you or the ones you love. What can you do?

Some would say—get out of the way—wait until they "hit bottom."

There is a better alternative—we need to find a way to "raise the bottom."

How do we "raise the bottom?"

1.
Stop rescuing your loved one

All too often we have covered up their irresponsible decisions—paid bail so they could get out of jail—paid delinquent bills, or the rent. We've believed their heart-stopping stories of tragedy.

"I cashed my check, and put the cash in my pocket. When I got home, the money was gone! I must have dropped it." They played the part so well—the tears, the frustration— "I was trying so hard to be responsible, and now I have nothing!"

Your heart of compassion goes out to them and you generously give to help them through to the next paycheck. You failed to see their story was a very convincing con job to get extra cash for drugs.

You "raise the bottom" for your loved one when you

say, "No," and allow them to face the painful consequences of their irresponsible actions.

2.
Tell them the truth

You help "raise the bottom" for your loved one by being truthful about their problems. We often have perfect insight in seeing the problems in strangers and other casual acquaintances.

But when it's your own family member—you want to believe the best—and you deceive yourself by saying, "Things really aren't all that bad. I'm sure things will get better soon."

You need to speak the truth—not in a torrent of frustration and rage—but firmly so the message is unmistakable. "You have a problem—you need to change— you need help. I can't change you. I won't make any more excuses for you. Help is available, but you must choose to get help."

Saying it one time usually won't break through the fog of confusion and delusion. Those who work in the field of addictions often see that it takes 30 or more such messages of truth before the person is ready to admit their need to get help.

Son almost starves to death

When a rebellious son wants to leave home, it's a painful time for the whole family, especially the parents. Clearly this is not the first sign of a problem in this family relationship.

The story told in Luke 15:11-32 shows an arrogant son demanding his share of the family inheritance even before his father dies.

He goes off and lives the party lifestyle until his money runs out. It's clear that his friends also abandon him.

He ends up feeding pigs, and the only food he gets is what the pigs leave. In spite of his desperate circumstances, no one helps him.

That's the good news of the story, because this painful mess is finally where he "hits bottom." He came to himself—reality finally broke through his delusion.

He accepted responsibility for his sins—his bad decisions, and decided to change.

The process of restoration started with his confession of his sin to God and then returning home to seek the forgiveness of his family.

He came back a changed man, free of the rebellious delusion that took him away from home.

3.
Don't make decisions for them

Some family members have forced their loved one into a program. Sometimes it works—after a few days in the program the addicted one realizes s/he needs to change and stay with this new path to healing and restoration.

But many people forced into programs leave prematurely and quickly return to their addiction.

Challenge your loved one to get help. Give them alternatives—speak the truth—but make it clear—they have to decide to change.

4.
Don't stop their pain

Some of us can walk away from a stranger who is in pain, homeless, dirty clothes—but when it is your own loved one—it's not so easy. But pain motivates change.

When we rescue our loved ones and prevent them from experiencing the painful consequences of their irresponsible decisions—we feed their delusion and extend their path to "hitting bottom." Instead of "raising the bottom," our wrong kind of help "lowers the bottom," making their destructive path even longer.

5.
Start early in life

Many of the addicted teens and young adults that come to Teen Challenge started their path to addiction even before they were a teenager. Disciplining children today is often viewed as taboo—an archaic holdover of past decades—some even call it child abuse.

But proper discipline is not child abuse. I remember when our children were 4 and 5 years old. Their disobedient behavior resulted in daily discipline. Sometimes my wife and I wondered out loud if the discipline was doing any good. We didn't see rapid change.

But as the children grew older—7, 8, 9 years old—we saw them become more obedient—not perfect. They learned early in life the painful consequences for disobedience.

Many teens and adults have never learned those lessons—instead they have experienced the "benefits" of irresponsibility. Discipline was rare. Selfish patterns became deeply ingrained as they headed into their teen years. Mom and Dad were there to rescue them whenever a crisis came.

The sooner in life you start applying proper discipline and consistent boundaries for your children—you "raise the bottom" for their trips down the road of irresponsibility.

If your child is 40 years old, you can't go back and change the past, but you can change the future.

6.
Get ready for emotional warfare

If you begin to "raise the bottom" and make your loved one face the painful consequences of their actions—with no more offers to rescue them—get ready for a flood of anger. "What kind of a Christian are you? You are supposed to help people when they have a crisis—especially family!"

Their anger may take the same path as little children being disciplined who scream—"I hate you!" If you can't stand their rejection and you cave in to their demands—you only "lower the bottom" and prolong their damage.

The words of Jesus on the cross can strengthen you when harsh words come at you. Jesus said, "Father, forgive them, for they do not know what they are doing." (Luke 23:34 NIV)

It was very painful for Jesus to do the right thing—to stay on the cross and pay the price for our salvation and healing. Are you willing to take the right path—the painful path—so you can "raise the bottom" for your loved ones?

If you truly love those close to you, then the loving thing to do may be very painful for a season—until your loved one turns from the path of destruction to God's path to freedom.

7.
Don't try to rush the process of recovery

Many times we have seen a person come to Teen Challenge and soon make dramatic progress toward healing and a whole new life.

"Raising the bottom" for our daughter

Our daughter made a lot of bad decisions regarding friends, and ended up on drugs. We often rescued her, paid bail, gave her money, even though we knew she was buying drugs.

We didn't want her to go back to her life of stealing. But she soon started stealing from us.

We finally realized we had to give her a hard choice—"Get help, or we will press charges and send you to jail."

She moved out, and soon got worse. She called and asked to come home, but we refused. We did not compromise.

Finally, with no place to go, her boyfriend in jail, she was willing to get help. She entered the Teen Challenge program. It wasn't easy, but we are so glad she is now getting real help.

—a grateful mother

The family is so excited—they haven't seen their loved one look so good for years. Relationships are restored, past hurts forgiven. Joyful tears and smiles replace the hurt, anger, and frustrations of the past.

We've seen families say, "Come home today, all is forgiven."

They fail to understand the path to recovery is more than putting on a few pounds and saying, "all is forgiven."

Family members need to carefully reinforce the process of restoration being taught your loved one.

If your addicted loved one is in Teen Challenge, you need to encourage your loved one to stay—and finish the program. That's not an easy task. Many students at Teen Challenge encounter problems and frustrations and want to leave.

A prayer for those with a loved one who has not "hit bottom"

God, s/he is in Your hands! Do whatever it takes to bring my loved one to a point of real change. Break through the delusion. I will not interfere with what You are doing. It really hurts, but I trust You, God.

Don't fall back into your old patterns of rescuing your loved one. You may get a phone call, "I want to come home. I don't need this program any more." They need to learn to face the problems and challenges in their life. They need to become consistent in making responsible decisions.

If you broke your leg and have a cast on it, you don't break it off after a few days because of the discomfort of the cast. The cast is restrictive—but it protects you during the healing process. Prematurely removing the cast does not speed the healing process.

In a similar way, do not let the promises of your loved one deceive you into taking the short cut on their path to healing. Your loved one may try to convince you that they are ready to leave—they don't need this program any more.

The most valuable help you can give is to require them to finish the program.

Many parents or wives have said, "If you leave the program before finishing it, you can't come home." This reality check has often been enough to make the addicted one reconsider—and stay in the program.

Your loved one is looking for the easy way out of these problems. Don't join the conspiracy of incomplete solutions.

There is perhaps nothing more painful than watching your loved one self destruct in the bondage of addiction. God offers freedom to each person, young or old, but He doesn't force His help on us.

You can't force your loved one to get help, but you can "raise the bottom" so they come face to face with reality sooner. It's a painful process, but "raising the bottom" will bring the benefits of healing so much faster.

Following are personal reflections on this issue of "Raising the Bottom," by Johnny Melendez, Canzada Edmonds, and Paul Patrick.

Personal Reflections on "Raise the Bottom"

Johnny Melendez

I did not have anyone encouraging me to change, except my mother. All my friends and family members accepted the fact that I was a drug addict. Some of them told me, "You are never going to change."

I didn't see much change in my friends. The choices they made to change took them down another road that was empty.

No one really tried to "raise the bottom" in my life. Deep down in my heart I knew that I needed to change— drastic change, radical change.

I did hit bottom, but what is bottom? It's a bottomless pit. There is no solid foundation at the bottom. My life continued to get worse and worse. There was no end to the bottom. No one really tried to "raise the bottom" in my life.

What ended up having a big influence on motivating me to change was the religious training I had received as a child. I knew there was a God, and maybe some day I would not be a drug addict.

I finally came to the point where I said, "I have to try something!" I knew I needed change. I didn't want to live in the streets anymore. I needed to get away from my friends and the streets where I lived. I was willing to try anything when I came to Teen Challenge. This is where God radically changed my life.

Personal Reflections on "Raise the Bottom"

Canzada Edmonds

I hit bottom on October 8, 1992, when I tried to commit suicide. For many years I could not identify with hitting bottom, because of living a life of deception. I was blind to hitting bottom. I could not identify with the concept—even when I lost jobs.

Then in October 1992, I was facing a life sentence–I had 5 felonies and 5 or 6 illegal drug arrests. They put this all together and said, "She's a career criminal, and we are going to lock her up for life." I said, "That's it! Before I go to jail for life, I'm going to take my own life."

But when I failed in my attempt to take my own life, at that point, I said, "I need some help." That was my bottom.

When I went back to court, Judge Burnette said, "I'm going to let you go to this Jesus program [Teen Challenge], because they say this program can help you. You go to this program, and you come back and see me when you finish this program."

Hitting bottom was not the magical turning point in my life, because there were lots of areas in my life where I needed to change. Hitting bottom did strip away some of the delusion I had been living with, but it did not fix all the problems in my life.

Even after I hit bottom, I had to realize that change was a process. There was so much hurt and pain I had suppressed for over 30 years. I had to come to grips with this—I had to identify the hurt and pain, and be willing to deal with it.

As I look back over the 27 years of addiction in my life before I hit bottom, very few people made any effort to call me to change.

I think that "raising the bottom" needs to start early in a person's addiction. When we meet those who are struggling, in the grips of addiction, it is very important that we embrace them, and show them real love. We also need to educate them on what the Bible says, because God is the one who is going to empower them to change. That's what took place in my life.

Personal Reflections on "Raise the Bottom"

Paul Patrick

I hit bottom in 2000, shortly after I was arrested for the third time—my third felony. At that point, my heroin habit was $200-300 a day. I was also taking methadone.

To me my bottom was to be humiliated. The worst thing that humiliated me was having inmates see me in this condition. I was smelling, with all the drugs coming out of my system. I was in the jail cell with people laughing at me, telling the corrections officers, "Get him out of this cell—he stinks, he smells."

Because they did not detox me, I started going into convulsions and seizures. I felt like everything was over. When I arrived at the hospital, the doctor thought I was dead.

That's when God did a miracle in my life as I shared in my testimony in this book.

When I was a small child, coming home from school, I would see the drug dealers in the neighborhood, others gambling, shooting dice. The drug dealers were well dressed and had a girlfriend. My single mom wasn't able to support us the way I wanted to be supported. There were 7 kids, and I was the youngest boy with one younger sister. I didn't get much after everyone got what they wanted.

I set out at an early age to make money in the streets. As a young teen I got involved in selling drugs. It wasn't long before I started using drugs.

I tried to hide my addiction. I thought I was hiding it from people—my girlfriend, my mother, everyone that was around me. In my state of mind it was foolishness to think that people didn't notice that I was getting high and going down. But no one stepped in and tried to get me to change.

Once in a while, someone would say, "You need to do something different with your life, or get your life together." But no one said anything that really stuck with me to make me think that I really needed to change.

Every time I was arrested, these were not messages that I should change. To me it was just a setback to selling drugs.

I figured, "I'll just do this time, and when I come home, my habit will be less."

All of my friends either used drugs or sold drugs. I had two friends who did get off drugs. One is a pastor, Spencer Wright. Before he changed, he was facing 25 years to life for murder. He went into prison as a "5 percenter" (a Muslim). While he was awaiting trial in Rikers Island, he gave his life to Jesus. For two years he served the Lord in Rikers Island.

After he got out, he would come around and try to speak to me, and I would try to hide from him. I didn't want to hear what he had to say.

My friend, Ruloff, also got off drugs. He's been clean off of drugs for 10 years now. But he still sold drugs, and he still did all the other things. I would look up to him and say, "I would like to be clean like that."

I remember as soon as I got arrested that last time, I said to myself, "I'm tired of this." I was facing my third felony. I realized I was either going to jail, or someone was going to kill me, or I'm going to kill somebody in jail. I felt this was the end of my life—that I was going to die in prison. But God had a plan to rescue me.

To be honest, if the bottom had been raised on me sooner, I believe I wouldn't have gone through all the stuff I did. I would have gotten help a lot sooner.

Why not "Raise the Bottom!"
Discussion Guide

The following questions can be used for your personal reflection on this topic, or it can be used as a guide for a group discussion. If this is used in a group setting, please understand that you are not required to disclose the specific details of past sins, failures, or personal experiences.

1. Read Luke 15:11-32. What were the experiences of the son on his way to "hitting bottom"? (see especially verses 12-16, 30-32)

2. What were the desperate conditions of the son when he "hit bottom"?

3. At the son's point of "hitting bottom" it says in verse 16 that no one helped him.

   A. What is your assessment of the fact that God voices no anger or rebuke towards those who did nothing to help this desperate young man?

   B. What change occurred in the life of this desperate young man? (verses 17-19)

4. In your life have you experienced a time when you "hit bottom?"

   A. What started you on the path of self-destruction?

   B. What false beliefs were you living with?

   C. What did it feel like to "hit bottom"?

   D. Did anyone offer the wrong kind of help which rescued you from the painful consequences of your actions, thus "lowering the bottom" and making yours a longer path to "hitting the bottom"?

   E. Did anyone do or say anything that helped "raise the bottom" in your life? Explain.

   F. How long was the recovery process in your life after you "hit bottom"?

5. Do you have a loved one on a path of destruction that has not yet "hit bottom"?

   A. What, if anything, have you said or done to try to rescue this person?

   B. How hard is it for you to let go of this person and let God do whatever it takes to bring your loved one to a place of change?

   C. What can you do to "raise the bottom" for your loved one?

48   Why not "Raise the Bottom!"

Freedom from 27 years of addiction

Canzada Edmonds 1995

I was ready to end my life. As I sat in that cold jail cell waiting to appear before the judge, I could not bear the thought of spending the rest of my life behind bars.

Society had labeled me as a career criminal and said I would never be anything. They said there was no hope for me. After 27 years of addiction I was caught up in that same despair.

When I awoke in the D.C. General Hospital, I was in even deeper despair—and full of anger. I had failed again.

I couldn't even kill myself. "Canzada, you are a hopeless case," I told myself.

The people at the hospital said, "We have to take you to court, because you have to face the judge." I said to myself, "Something is really wrong with me."

Childhood memories flooded back. "You'll never amount to anything," had been seared into my memory by my father. He was a functional alcoholic who never lived at home, yet he was able to father 14 boys and three girls.

Mom was never there either. She and her boyfriend lived a few blocks from where I grew up with my grandparents. About the only time she came by was to drop off another baby. She would tap me on my head, saying, "Hi, how are you doing?" and then she would leave. Anger grew within me—all I wanted was a mother who would love me.

Not finding love at home, I turned to friends at school, but as a young teen, I found myself victimized by betrayal again. This time the consequence was an unwanted pregnancy.

Everybody was asking me, "Who is the baby's father?" I felt a lot of shame and guilt, but I never told my grandparents or my brothers what really happened.

I felt worthless, I felt dirty. I started using PCP heavily, hoping it would end my pregnancy—it didn't. My son Sterling was born, and one month later he died of pneumonia.

Losing touch with reality

My son's death pushed me over the brink. I began to lose touch with reality, and ended up in a mental institution. I was only 15. Four months later I was back home, back in school—and back into drugs.

The next twenty-four years saw my life twist and turn with more pain and "success." Getting a good job came easy for me. I soon developed another addiction—shoplifting. What started with small things soon led to stealing mink coats and anything my customers wanted. My heroin habit rose to $1,000 a day.

I got caught stealing and went to jail several times. I tried methadone treatment for 11 years, but nothing set me free. With five major felonies on my record, the judge was ready to send me away for life. That's when I decided to end it all in that cell block on October 8, 1994. But even my suicide attempt failed.

The beginnings of hope

But some Christians at the methadone clinic were praying for me. One of them was a graduate of Teen Challenge. She spoke to the judge on my behalf.

The judge didn't allow the prosecutor to speak, and he didn't allow my attorney to speak. But he looked at me and said, "I really believe there is some help for you, so I am going to send you to this "Jesus Program."

At that time I didn't know anything about Jesus, and I had no idea what kind of a program this Teen Challenge was. But today I truly believe God works behind the scenes to help us in our time of need.

The judge said, "I'm sending you to Teen Challenge for two years, and then I want you to come back and see me. Then I will decide what to do with you regarding these charges."

On January 30, 1995, I found myself at Teen Challenge. Looking back now, I can say this was the best thing that ever happened to me. But that cold day in January, I arrived in Brooklyn, New York, a confused person— desperate, stubborn, and suspicious of others.

My mind was messed up. I had no hope. I believed I was going to die an addict. I also carried in my heart an attitude of prejudice.

When I came that day, I arrived with a lot of stolen merchandise, because I was addicted to stealing as well as drugs. I had trunks full of stolen clothing, even mink coats. I don't know where I thought I was going!

They said I was going away for two years, so I said to myself, "I need to be well prepared." So before I left D.C., I made it my business to go to Neiman Marcus, and Lord and Taylor to pick me up a couple of mink coats and a whole new set of clothes.

After I had been at Teen Challenge for a short time, one

of the staff, Marian Washington, approached me and said, "Something is not right. Where did you get all these clothes?"

"What do you mean?" I replied. "These are my clothes. I brought them."

They told me the clothes were stolen and I would have to get rid of them, because they would bring more problems into my life.

I said, "These people are crazy! What's wrong with you? If I get rid of all these clothes, what am I going to wear?"

Marian said, "We have some clothes for you to wear."

"I'm not going to wear somebody's hand-me-downs," I responded angrily. "I'm just not going to do that!"

"OK," she said, "just take your time. In the morning, come back and tell us how the Lord is—"

"The Lord!" I exploded. At that time I didn't have a relationship with God.

The next morning the staff asked me, "Has the Holy Spirit dealt with you about this?"

"What are you talking about—the Holy Spirit?"

I responded, because I had no idea how the Holy Spirit was working in my life.

But that night I came to the staff and said, "I do want to change my life, so I am going to give you all my stolen goods." Everything I had brought was stolen. I had nothing left when I turned it all in, including the notebook paper and pens and pencils which I had stolen. Even the trunks I had used to bring all my clothes to Brooklyn were stolen. And I said, "God, I just want You to help me."

That same addiction was still in my life, and I took it down to the "Blessing room" where all the hand-me-down clothes were stored. I started to steal clothes out of the blessing room like I was in a department store.

I was also getting in trouble with the men in the men's program. The rules prohibited us from talking to the men, but I was passing notes, and talking to the men through the heating vent in the bathroom. Sure enough, I got caught.

My counselor went to Dotty Bolger, the Program Director, and said, "I give up. I can't handle Canzada. She lies to me. I just don't know what to do with her."

So Dotty took away my counselor. I pleaded with Dotty, "I need a counselor, I need someone to talk to, because I've got lots of problems."

"No," Dotty replied, "we are going to let the Holy Spirit deal with you."

"These people are really crazy," I thought to myself. They are going to let some spirit deal with me! Something is wrong with this place!

The Laundry Room

For my discipline they assigned me to work in the laundry room in the basement of the women's home. The counselors wouldn't counsel me. At that time I had to call on God. I said, "God, I don't know where you are, but they say I have to be here and I have to wait for you to help me. So I'm waiting for you. I do want to get this relationship with you that they talk about—but I don't know what it is."

So I stayed in the laundry room and read the Bible. Weeks passed, and I stayed in the laundry room and read the Bible. Normally they assign new jobs to students every two or three weeks. But not for me. Ninety days later, I was still in the laundry room, still reading the Bible.

The staff could see that I was growing, but I didn't see it. And when I came out of the laundry room, I had a genuine personal relationship with God!

The staff at Teen Challenge showed me the love of Jesus, and slowly the wounds from the past began to heal.

For the first time in 26 years, I revealed my secret of being raped.

Back when I was a young teen and in junior high school, I really liked Kevin; he was really cool and handsome. One Friday morning he asked me to cut class and go to his house for lunch. When I got there it was nothing like I imagined. He had six other guys waiting. I was gang raped.

Out of that experience I became pregnant. From that day on I hated men. I hated my baby when he was born because he was a boy. I prayed to God—not knowing who He was—I prayed that my son would die. When my son Sterling died a month later, that bitterness just went all the deeper in my heart.

Now 26 years later, God began to do a work of healing in my life. The hatred of men was replaced with godly love. And today I can say, I love my brothers in the Lord.

The daily Bible study classes and required scriptures to memorize helped me to discover a whole new way of living. God began to clear away the confusion and the hatred.

When I first came to Teen Challenge, my mind was so confused that it took me three months to memorize one short verse—Luke 1:37, "With God, nothing is impossible." But I began to stand on that promise in my life, and I still stand on it today.

After using drugs for 27 years, I had no hope. But God was now giving me hope, peace, joy, and love. I experienced a peace that surpasses all understanding, a love that can go beyond measure, a joy that no man can remove, and hope that is unlimited. With God's help, my whole way of thinking was changed.

Learning to like myself

For a long time I had not been able to look in the mirror and like what I saw. I learned that God loved me even though my past life was so ugly.

When I came to Teen Challenge I had a real problem with lying and deception. In the past I would always lie to keep myself out of trouble. But God taught me how to tell the truth and experience the freedom that goes with it.

With Jesus as the director of my life, I no longer crave for drugs or hold bitterness to others. God has given me godly character—something I never imagined I would have.

A life with a future

On June 8, 1996, I completed the Teen Challenge residential program and returned to Washington, D.C., to work. One year later I returned to Teen Challenge in Brooklyn, New York, this time as a staff. I loved working with the ladies coming off the streets. They were coming with the same despair and hopelessness I once had, bound by drug addiction and hurts from the past.

What a delight it was to share with them the joyful news that Jesus has the power to change their lives. I can't think of anything else I would rather do.

In January 2000, God called me back to Washington, D.C., and I began to work as an addictions counselor in a secular program. God gave me favor with my supervisor, and I was able to pray with my clients. And then I began to lead a group session that was spiritually based, where I was able to share the word of God with them.

Today I continue to serve the Lord. Do I have trials and problems? Oh yes! But the lessons I learned at Teen Challenge continue to point me to the right decisions in responding to these situations.

Today Canzada Edmonds Twyman is happily married and living in the Atlanta area. She has completed a masters degree in Human Services. She is a licensed evangelist and also serves as the founder and executive director of The Divine Exchange ministry, reaching out to drug addicts in methadone clinics and on the streets, showing them how they can find help through Jesus.

A Miracle for a Muslim before salvation

Paul Patrick 2000

I had been arrested again and sent to Riker's Island jail in Queens, New York. This time I was facing 10 years in prison. But an even greater concern at that moment was my addiction. I was getting sicker by the minute because my body was going through withdrawal from drugs.

I was twenty years into my addiction to heroin. I was also addicted to methadone four years. When I got arrested, the police wouldn't give me any medication to detox from the drugs I was using.   I had been in jail before, and they were tired of seeing me again.

As I was kicking "cold turkey," I started to have seizures, and I couldn't breathe.   They finally transferred me to Bellevue Hospital, but when I arrived, I had no vital signs.

They were trying to get blood, but there was no pulse. They went up my spine, they stuck a needle in my neck, in my jugular vein, trying to get blood. My body was getting cold. The doctor soon gave up, and left the room.

But God put two angels in the hospital that day. Two

of the nurses who had been working on me began to pray. One grabbed my hand and began calling on the name of Jesus.

I can't explain how I knew what was going on, but I was aware that they were praying for me, and I was getting really angry. I had been raised a Muslim, and I didn't want anyone praying to Jesus for me.

But since I was in a coma, and for all practical purposes dead, or close to it, there was nothing I could do about their prayers for me. For over 20 minutes they continued to cry out to Jesus.

My body started getting warm, and as I started coming out of it, the nurses got all excited. They called for the doctor, and the room got all crowded with people.

Right there at the bedside these nurses led me to Jesus. Much like Paul in the New Testament, I had my dramatic "Damascus Road" experience. I prayed to receive Christ. And what a dramatic turn of events this brought into my life!

Two days later my lawyer came to the hospital and told me that I had to be released from police custody. There is a law in New York, that once you are arrested, you must be presented before a judge within 188 hours, or be released. Because of going through withdrawals from my addiction and ending up in the hospital, I had exceeded that time, so I was released on my own recognizance. I was not required to arrange for my bail which had originally been set at $10,000.

I knew that I would soon be standing before that judge, still facing 10 years in prison. Someone gave me the phone number of Times Square Church where Dave Wilkerson was the pastor. They referred me to Teen Challenge in Brooklyn.

So I decided to check into Teen Challenge. In my mind I said, "I'll go into this program to make it look good when I go back into court. The judge might have mercy on me because of being in a program—especially a Christian program."

I had no idea what Teen Challenge was like. At first it was hard, because it was so close to my old neighborhood. As I was walking down the block from the home where we stayed to the main center, I would see a lot of people I knew.

But I soon discovered the prayer room at Teen Challenge, in the basement of the men's home. I went into the prayer room after being there for two weeks, and I just cried out to the Lord. The Lord really touched me, and He began to speak to me, and my life began to change.

Even though I had been a Muslim all my life, I knew that Jesus was real—especially after what happened in that hospital room. Once the Lord really touched me and the nurses led me to Christ—that was it. My mind was fixed that I would leave the Muslim faith.

As a Muslim, I never had a relationship with Allah. It was just formalities, I was going through the motions with no relationship.

But Jesus became so real to me. I spoke to Him in prayer, I heard from Him. As I read the Bible I saw the promises and the miraculous things. The Bible came alive to me. This was a big difference from the Muslim faith, where everything I read there had never really helped me. It was just words on a page, and I was just following others. As a Muslim, I had really been into the militant faction as well.

When I came to Teen Challenge, I faced a lot of struggles, especially in the first few weeks. But God spoke to me and told me He was calling me into the ministry. I determined in my heart that there was no turning back for me. My heart and mind were fixed and made up.

I had visions from the Lord showing me the blessings I would experience in my life if I would follow Him. Although I did not have them yet, God showed me my wife and children. He also showed me sickness and disease that would come on me and my family if I chose the path of disobedience.

Every day at Teen Challenge we were going to the classes and learning how to live the Christian life. I began to have a hunger for the Word of God through these classes. The whole curriculum made me learn so much about myself. I soon realized that the problems in my life were much deeper than the drugs I had used for 20 years. I learned that there was deep rooted sin in my life that God had to help me overcome.

I started to have compassion for other people, and have love for others. My speech was curbed—I no longer had curse words coming out of my mouth. I learned how to submit to authority right here at Teen Challenge.

Whatever work I did, I worked as unto the Lord. My relationship got so close to God. Others could see the change that I couldn't see.

There were two low points for me that almost pulled me out of Teen Challenge. The first was the death of a close friend of mine while I was in Brooklyn. I had only been in Teen Challenge for a couple of months, and I wanted to go to his funeral. But my leaders would not let me go. I was really angry and I could not understand it at the time, but as I look back now, it was definitely for my benefit.

Several months later after I had transferred to the Teen Challenge Training Center in Rehrersburg, Pennsylvania, one of my family members died. Again, I was not able to attend the funeral. It was hard, but the Lord kept me at Teen Challenge. I learned through these dark times that God is faithful and able to keep you. God will give you a way of escape when temptation comes. Now that I am more mature in Christ I understand the reasons why I was not allowed to go home.

From the day I entered Teen Challenge, I knew I would have to go before the judge to settle the charges I was facing. After a few weeks at Teen Challenge, I decided that I wanted to go before the judge and get this settled. I was convinced I would have to do time in prison, and I wanted to get it done with.

At my request, the staff at Teen Challenge would call up and talk to the District Attorney for me. For some reason they kept putting my case on hold. I kept asking for a court date.

I was planning to plead guilty so I could get a lesser charge, maybe three or five years. I was willing to do that with no problem because I already had three felonies on my record. If I got convicted of this one I would have been a three time loser.

These phone calls continued right up until it was time for me to transfer to the Teen Challenge Training Center in

Pennsylvania. But it was always the same answer—your case has been delayed. I had been at Pennsylvania for a month when my lawyer called. "I've got great news for you! All the charges against you have been dropped. So you don't need to stay at that Teen Challenge program. You can leave right now."

"I know you won't understand," I told my Jewish lawyer, "but I have to finish this program. I know who did this for me."

The whole time I was in Brooklyn I said to myself, "If they dismiss my case, I will leave." So the Lord waited until I got to Teen Challenge in Pennsylvania before He released my court case. And I was ready to stay the next seven months and finish the program and get all that God had for me.

In the days that followed, God spoke to me again, and told me that He was calling me into the pastoral ministry. The Lord told me that He was going to send me back into the community to do evangelism.

God showed me the blessings that would come. He showed me how I would be involved in ministry in the urban housing projects area, coming between gang members, and bringing them together. He showed me bringing other Muslims to the Lord. Today I can report that this has already come to pass. I've already seen two of my Muslim friends come to the Lord.

While I was at Teen Challenge in Pennsylvania, God started opening doors for me to go into prisons and do ministry there. The last three months in Teen Challenge, the Lord put on my heart to go to Bible college and be trained even more for the ministry. God said I was not ready to go back home.

God brought some pastors into my life, and as I shared with them the calling God had placed on my life, they offered to send me to Bible college. They paid for the three years of my Bible college training.

Even as a student in Bible college, God opened many doors for me to minister. Even though I had not obtained any certificates, ordination, or degrees, the Lord allowed me to preach in all types of churches: Methodist, Baptist, Pentecostal, Church of God in Christ, Assemblies of God and many other congregations. God sent me all over and I learned so much. It is just amazing.

Even more amazing were the doors of ministry God opened in the jails and prisons in Pennsylvania. As soon as I began Bible college, I was given the opportunity to preach in many prisons in the state of Pennsylvania. During the three years I was in Bible college, I spoke in almost every county jail in Pennsylvania. I have a special love for this ministry because of the time I spent in prison and the way I was raised.

When I was growing up on the streets of Brooklyn, and in prison, I never met anyone who was a Christian. I never saw an evangelist coming into the housing projects where I lived. Oh, yes, I did see Jehovah's Witnesses and Mormons.

I grew up in an environment of drugs. I was the seventh of eight children. My father wasn't there, so I was raised by my mother. It was hard. I was the second youngest. We didn't have much in the house—we lived in a three bedroom apartment—all nine of us.

By the time things got down to me and my little sister, there wasn't much left—food, clothing, whatever. So when I got to be 13 years old, I said to myself, "I'm going to take care of myself and my little sister." So I took to the streets—attracted to drug dealers, driving around in their fancy cars, flashing money. I started selling drugs, supporting my sister and I. My mother didn't know what was going on.

By the time I was 16, I was doing really well. I had people under me selling drugs. That same year I started to use heroin. It started slow, but it just took over me, and I stayed in that addiction almost 20 years.

There was a church right across the street from where I lived. The church people would talk about me, but they never invited me into the church. One night I got shot right across the street from that church. On another occasion when I was 16, I got stabbed in my lungs right across the street from the church. I never knew that peace was just inside those doors.

All the time I spent in prison, I never heard about Jesus. And that is why I am so interested in prison ministry, because I didn't receive that while I was in prison. I was 34 years old before I met those nurses who prayed for me and pointed me to the life Jesus had for me.

I see the hand of God on my life, and today I want to do whatever He wants me to do.

Enabling

Are you offering the wrong kind of help to your loved ones?

One of the most common problems I see in Christians today is confusion about how to help a loved one who has a problem. Offering the wrong kind of help, they end up feeding the problem—and working against what God is trying to do in the life of their loved one.

Every day we get calls and letters from people asking, "How can we help our son or daughter or grandchild who is using drugs, running with the wrong friends, rebelling against their parents?"

Many are godly parents who have prayed and fasted for their child—yet they watch painfully as their child continues down a path of rebellion and destruction. One mother told me, "I pray for my children, but why is God so slow to answer?"

So what can parents or grandparents do to help their loved ones?

Stop enabling!

What is enabling?

Enabling is offering the wrong kind of help. Enabling is rescuing your loved one so they don't experience the painful consequences of their irresponsible decisions.

Enabling is anything that stands in the way of persons experiencing the natural consequences of their own behavior.

Galatians 6:7-8 speaks to Christians about this with simple—blunt truth: "Do not be deceived: God cannot be mocked. A man reaps what he sows. The one who sows to please his sinful nature, from that nature will reap destruction; the one who sows to please the Spirit, from the Spirit will reap eternal life."

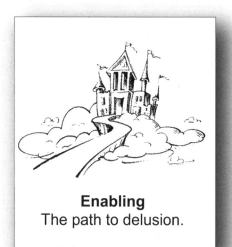

Enabling
The path to delusion.

God's word here is specific—Christians— don't be deceived! Your own children can deceive you when it comes to this scripture. We are willing to accept this verse when it comes to sinners living around us. But when it comes to our own children—are we willing to let God be in control?

Many parents simply cannot stand by and watch their child suffer pain from bad decisions—so they rescue them. One grandmother told me, "I can understand that my alcoholic daughter needs to experience the painful consequences of her actions—but I cannot stand to see my little grandchildren suffer—they are innocent little ones." So she "helps" them.

At first glance it seems the loving thing to do—to help the innocent grandchildren. But do we "mock God" when we do that? Are we not getting in God's way? There are no simple answers.

If God specifically speaks to you to reach out and offer specific help—then by all means do it! But all too often we offer help, not because God specifically spoke to us, but because we think it is the right thing to do.

Some parents want to minimize the damage in the lives of their children. The result—they become part of the deception. A father said, "I make sure my teenage daughter has a condom when she goes out on a date. I don't want her to get AIDS." He is deceiving himself and his daughter—and the man she is dating. Safe sex? Safe sin?

When we give anyone the impression there is a "safe way to sin," we are mocking God. Sin always causes destruction. When we step in and rescue people from the consequences of their sin, we only push our loved one farther down the path of delusion and destruction.

Are you offering the wrong kind of help?

So how do we know if we are offering the wrong kind of help? One test is to ask—does my help prevent this person from experiencing the natural consequences of their irresponsible decisions?

Another test—The help you have been giving—is it actually helping? Is your loved one changing? Look at their actions—is there clear evidence of becoming a responsible godly person? Or is your loved one caught up in another crisis—continuing down the path of destruction? You've got to face facts—stop living in the land of wishful thinking.

Parents often start enabling their children when they are very young. When our son was 13 years old, and the new school year had started, he forgot to take his lunch. So I dropped it off at school on my way to work. A few days later it happened again—then again.

My wife and I decided to stop rescuing Tim in this area of his life. We told him, "From now on you have full responsibility for your lunch. You must pack it yourself. You must remember to take it to school.

"If you forget, you go without lunch. We will not bring it to school. We forbid you to borrow money at school to pay for it." (The school had a generous loan policy for students who forgot their lunch money.)

In just a few days, Tim forgot his lunch. A few days later it happened again. So do you think he changed and became really responsible with his lunch? No—there was no quick lesson that led to maturity.

Some days he packed his lunch and left it setting on the counter. Other days he forgot his quarter for buying milk.

His best friend at school often shared his lunch with Tim when Tim forgot his. Yes—there are plenty of other enablers ready to help your loved one when you stick to your commitment to stop enabling.

One day Tim packed his lunch and walked out the door leaving it on the kitchen counter. That night I asked Tim how lunch was, because I knew he had left his lunch at home that day.

He had remembered to bring his quarter for milk, he told me. As he slowly drank it in the cafeteria, another student asked—"who wants my apple—I don't want it." Tim grabbed it quickly.

Then his choir teacher came through handing out

cupcakes to all the choir—including Tim—as a special way of expressing appreciation for a recent concert they had done.

Finally the cafeteria staff called, "Free seconds for the leftovers!" and Tim got a free hamburger. It's amazing how the Lord provides! —the Lord?

Well, so much for the lessons on experiencing hunger pains all afternoon in hopes of teaching our son to be responsible!

Throughout the rest of the school year, Patty and I stuck to our commitment—Tim didn't starve to death, even though he forgot his lunch numerous times.

What I want you to know is that we felt pain every time we saw him forget his lunch. Just a few simple words from us, and he could have avoided hunger. But we would have been reinforcing his irresponsible behavior.

Just to let you know—today our son is actively involved in ministry in an inner city church in Detroit. And yes—he has learned much about being a responsible person.

All too often parents keep rescuing their children when the problems are little problems. Before you know it your children are teenagers or young adults, still making irresponsible decisions, and parents are still rescuing them— but now we are talking about big problems.

A grandmother wrote me this past week about her grandson who is using drugs. "Is there information somewhere on what parents must do to deal with children on drugs?" she asked.

I called and she told me a sad story of her son, a professor at a Christian college, married to a wonderful Christian woman—they have three children. Two are doing great, but one son is using drugs. He failed his first year of college, and is now living back at home with his parents.

They give their son money to buy drugs, and they are making the payments on his car. Mom's reluctant to see him get a job, because then he would have more money to buy drugs and get in more trouble.

They are praying for a miracle—but they are feeding an addiction—all in the name of love.

If their son is going to change his way of living, then the parents must stop offering the wrong kind of help. I could give story after story of those who have come to Teen Challenge—many decided to get help only after their family stopped enabling them.

If you stop enabling, get ready for more trouble

When you stop enabling—when you stop offering the wrong kind of help—you have no guarantee of quick solutions in the life of your loved one.

Your loved one may become very angry at you—and for a "good" reason. You've stopped rescuing them! Now they are beginning to feel the painful consequences of their irresponsible decisions.

He or she may attack you, "What kind of a Christian are you! Doesn't the Bible say you are supposed to help people in need?" They will use any argument to heap guilt and condemnation on you—but don't receive that into your heart.

You must stand on the facts—especially if you have a tender heart, easily moved by emotional, passionate messages. You must continue to rehearse the facts.

Pain motivates change

When we rescue a loved one from the painful consequences of irresponsible decisions, we often slow down their motivation to change.

Are you afraid to trust God?

When you stop enabling your loved one it may involve letting your loved one go farther down the path of destruction. You may be saying, "I can't bear to see my daughter in such pain and danger. She might get killed! And then I would have her death on my hands. I can't let that happen!"

Are you afraid to trust God? Is your God big enough to keep track of your child headed down the path of rebellion? Is your God too busy to give personal attention to the needs of your loved one?

The prodigal son's father was not an enabler

Place your hope in the story of the prodigal son recorded in Luke 15. We see a powerful picture of a father who did not enable his son. He allowed him to leave home, knowing the son would soon waste the inheritance he had worked a lifetime to save.

If you have read the story you know the rebellious son spent everything he had, ended up in a pig pen, and died. Right? No—but isn't that what many people fear will happen to their child—if I let him go down that path, and don't stop him, he's going to die!

So what brought the rebellious son to a place of being ready to change? He ended up in the pig pen, and went to his psychiatrist and worked through all his childhood traumas and found the answers—No! I'm not against godly counseling, but counseling is not always the answer.

Luke says he ended up in the pig pen. He was so hungry that he was tempted to eat what the pigs left when they had finished eating. I was raised on a small farm in Wisconsin. We raised a few pigs, and many days I fed them. But never was I tempted to eat what they left! This young man must have been really desperate!

Who has the problem?

Concerned parents were frustrated with their son, now in his 30s, still living at home. He was refusing to change.

The parents finally sought the help of a professional counselor. They poured out their frustrations regarding their son who refused to believe he had a problem.

After listening to their story, the counselor said, "I agree with your son. He doesn't have a problem. You've taken it away from him. Give it back to him! Make him take responsibility for his decisions and his life."

God's help
for rebellious children

Now comes the good news from the pig pen—Luke says, "and no one helped him." (verse 16)

God did not condemn anyone for failing to help this desperate young man in the pig pen. No thundering judgment from heaven toward those who did nothing.

Where is the father? Why isn't he out looking for his son? Doesn't he care that his son is starving to death?

The father is at home—waiting in painful peace. Peace because he has committed his son into God's hands. Painful peace, because he hurts for his son who is hurting. But he waits for God's solution. He's not going to get in God's way.

So what is happening to the son? Since "no one helped him," he's experiencing the full pain of his irresponsible decisions.

The very next words point to the truth, the power, and the effectiveness of God's way of helping stubborn children caught up in a destructive lifestyle. All alone in the pigpen, it says, "He came to his senses."

"How many of my father's hired men have food to

spare, and here I am starving to death! I will set out and go back to my father and say to him: Father, I have sinned against heaven and against you. I am no longer worthy to be called your son; make me like one of your hired men." (vs. 17-19)

Who can take credit for helping the son in his greatest time of need? No one! At the point of starving to death—he came to his senses. At the lowest point in his life—God still knew exactly where he was.

The son made a choice—the right choice—that put him on the path to restoration—the path to life!

When he meets his father, true repentance comes with his words, "Father, I have sinned against heaven and against you." (vs. 21) He takes personal responsibility for his past actions. It's time for joyful peace and a celebration!

Desperate, but not repentant

But some children want to come home—in desperation—but not like the prodigal son. A pastor's wife came to my office one day, deeply troubled. Two years earlier her son had been a senior in high school, rebellious, failing his classes, using drugs. The parents gave their son three rules:

➢ No using drugs in the house.

> ➢ On school nights he must be home by midnight.

> ➢ If he did not attend school, he must get a job.

Disgusted with such outrageous rules, the son left home and stayed with different friends until he wore out his welcome. Now two years later he was calling his mom saying, "I want to come home."

She was deeply troubled that if she said, "No," she would be failing to show God's agape love—unconditional love to her son. I asked her, "Has your son agreed to your rules."

"No," she said, "he's given us his own set of rules."

I assured her that she was doing the right thing to say "No" to her unrepentant son. He was still looking for someone to rescue him from the painful consequences of his irresponsible decisions.

When you stop enabling your loved one, you have no guarantee of a quick transformation in the life of your loved one. When you look at the story of the prodigal son's father——when he offered the right kind of help, his son went from bad to worse before things got better.

Learning to be at peace with God

You can rest in the peace that God has the address of your loved ones, no matter how deep they are in sin. His love far surpasses your love. He knows what will work best to bring your loved ones to that point of change.

You've got to trust God—even when things are going from bad to worse. Stop offering the wrong kind of help. Stop feeding the problem. Stop being deceived. Stop mocking God. Trust Him.

Place your hope in Him

In Galatians chapter 6, Paul goes on to give words of encouragement after challenging us not to be deceived into ignoring God's law of sowing and reaping. "Let us not become weary in doing good, for at the proper time we will

God is not an enabler

God will not offer the wrong kind of help to you or your loved ones. He will not rescue you from the consequences of your irresponsible decisions.

He will not help you in such a way that would feed the problems in your life. Even though He sees clearly all your problems, He still loves you deeply.

reap a harvest if we do not give up. Therefore, as we have opportunity, let us do good to all people, especially to those who belong to the family of believers." (Galatians 6:9-10)

Two times Paul refers to "doing good" to people. I think it would be very appropriate to say that he is referring to offering the right kind of help—not enabling. Let us not become weary of offering the right kind of help, which in some cases is offering "tough love."

Let us not enable others, especially those who belong to the family of believers. The promise is clear to us—if we continue to offer the right kind of help, we will reap a harvest—a good harvest. If we offer the wrong kind of help we will reap a harvest of pain, problems, regret, and more disappointments.

Jesus is ready to help us offer the right kind of help. He offers to give us wisdom to make the difficult decisions. He also stands ready and waiting with open arms to help our loved ones who really need His help.

Characteristics of the enabler

1. **Works for self-improvement.** If I were a better parent my son wouldn't use drugs. If I were a better wife, my husband wouldn't run around with other women.

2. **Changes the environment to accommodate the person with the problem.** Let's change schools and get our child away from those trouble-makers.

3. **Takes on the whole world in defense of their loved one.** The whole legal system is corrupt, and my child is getting the unjust treatment.

4. **Their pain increases.** Because the problems are not being resolved in the life of their loved one.

5. **Communication deteriorates.** The issues are not being resolved, defenses are high, and delusion is still present in both the enabler and the loved one with the problems.

6. **Enabling is habit-forming.** The enabler offers the same help as in the past without assessing its effectiveness or appropriateness for today. The enabler may get such a sense of personal satisfaction from helping that s/he does not stop to assess whether the help is helping or hurting.

Following are personal reflections on this issue of "Enabling: Are you offering the wrong kind of help to your loved ones," by Canzada Edmonds and Paul Patrick.

Personal Reflections on "Enabling"
Canzada Edmonds

I have 13 brothers, and for 2 of my brothers, I was their pride and joy. They would do anything for me. They planted that seed at a very early age—that anything I wanted, I could get it.

My brother, Ronnie, was a thief. He would always tell me, "You can just take it." The idea of shop-lifting was planted in me long before I started using drugs.

I left home at the age of 15. I wanted to have my own money. So a friend showed me how to steal mink coats and other expensive clothes. I learned how to do it well. I built a very nice clientele with doctors and lawyers. I was able to establish a little business in the basement of my house. In one sense, all of my clients were enablers, because they were helping me do wrong.

I worked a job in the medical field. I was a "functional" drug addict. I worked every day. With my paycheck, I would pay my bills. However, I would also "boost"—my money from shoplifting would go into my drug life. So I thought I really had it all together, because I had this fantastic plan. But I was deceived.

Even in my job at the hospital, my supervisor would encourage me to get a few items. She would say, "You are such a good worker, I will be glad when you get off these drugs." But on the other hand she would say to me, "Could you get me an Ellen Tracey suit?"

There would be days when I could not come to work, and I would still get paid for the day. Because my supervisor was getting something out of the deal, she thought she was helping me. Instead she was enabling me.

When I was having a bad day with my boosting business, I could go to my drug dealer, and he would supply my drugs. This guy would enable me with drugs. I knew I could always get drugs from him.

The lawyers I used were also enabling me. They would call me and I was providing them with Bisarge suits and Georgio Armoni suits. I didn't have to pay them with cash to keep my freedom.

My whole circle of relationships was filled with people who were enabling me.

There were only two people who were not like these

other people. My probation officer always tried to talk to me, but I was always in so much deception, and getting high—it was going in one ear and out the other. The other person was Catherine Baega, a counselor at a detox center I was in. She showed real love to me and introduced me to Teen Challenge. That is where I finally found freedom from my addiction and other life-controlling problems. God has truly changed my life!

Personal Reflections on "Enabling"
Paul Patrick

My mother was definitely an enabler in my life. I remember as a teenager getting my mother in trouble with the New York Housing Authority, jeopardizing her home because I got arrested on the property. They made her sign papers that I was not allowed in her house any more. She would be thrown out—evicted—if I was caught in her house again.

But she kept letting me back in the house, even though she could lose the apartment. When I was in my 20s, I got arrested again in her apartment. This time they handcuffed my mother, and everyone else in the apartment. The police found guns and drugs in the house. This time they were ready to throw her out of the apartment. Yet she still let me back in the house again.

This was definitely enabling me to continue my life of selling and using drugs, especially in the neighborhood. If she had not let me stay there, I had no other place in the neighborhood where I could stay. No one would have let me into their apartment.

I'm not saying she was to blame for me selling drugs, but if she had shown me tough love, I probably would not have stayed on to sell drugs in the neighborhood.

The methadone program also worked as an enabler in my life. When I got shot in 1997, I wasn't able to get out and buy my drugs and sell them. At that point I got on the methadone program thinking it would help me from having to go out and buy heroin. But once I got on the methadone program, I was still using heroin.

One of the rules of the methadone program was that I was not to get high on cocaine or heroin. Once they found out that I was using heroin or cocaine, they would raise my methadone dosage.

I started in the methadone program at 30 milligrams and went up to 100 milligrams. For a short time the 100 milligrams gave me a better high than the 30. But soon my body grew accustomed to the hundred.

I knew I wouldn't get in trouble with the methadone clinic if I came in and tested positive for heroin or cocaine— they would just give me more methadone. But the down side of this was that with my increasing use of methadone, I had to take more heroin to get high.

I think enabling is a big problem in almost every addict's life. Every addict has someone who is helping them do the things they are doing. I believe my addiction would have stopped a lot sooner if someone would have offered me tough love.

Enabling

Discussion Guide

The following questions can be used for your personal reflection on this topic, or it can be used as a guide for a group discussion. If this is used in a group setting, please understand that you are not required to disclose the specific details of past sins, failures, or personal experiences.

1. What are some examples of enabling (offering the wrong kind of help) you have seen in your own family or friends?

2. A. In your own life—in the past or present—were there people who enabled you? Who rescued you from the consequences of your irresponsible decisions?

    B. What impact did that "help" have on your life?

3. A. Is there a family member or friend that you are presently enabling?

    B. If yes, how is your help rescuing them?

    C. What do you fear will be the consequences if you do not give this person help?

4. Some people feel guilt for not helping others in need. How easy is it for others to use guilt to get you to help them?

5. Read Proverbs 3:5-6. Some battle with the fear: "If I don't help my loved ones then something worse will happen to them—they might even die!"

   A. How big an issue is this fear in your life?

   B. How difficult is it for you to trust God as you stop enabling your loved ones?

6. Some have a difficult time determining if their help is the wrong kind of help (enabling), or if it is the right kind of help.

   A. How hard is it for you to determine if you are offering the wrong kind of help?

   B. What scriptures can you stand on to help you in making Godly decisions about what kind of help to give your loved ones?

Scriptures for further study:
Proverbs 1,   Luke 15,   Galatians 6:7-10

How you can experience a miracle in your life today

This book tells how Johnny, Ralph, Canzada and Paul discovered a whole new relationship with Jesus Christ. You also can experience this relationship with Jesus.

1. Who is Jesus?

Jesus asked, "Who do you say I am?" Simon Peter answered, "You are the Christ, the Son of the Living God." Matthew 16:15-16

2. Is Jesus the only way to God?

Jesus answered, "I am the way and the truth and the life. No one comes to the Father except through me." John 14:6

3. What if I haven't really done any big sins?

God's truth applies whether you've sinned a lot or a little.

"There is no one righteous, not even one; there is no one who understands, no one who seeks God." Romans 3:10-11

4. How can I be saved?

If you confess with your mouth, "Jesus is Lord," and believe in your heart that God raised him from the dead, you will be saved. Romans 10:9

5. How do I know God loves me?

For God so loved the world that he gave his one and only Son, that whoever believes in him shall not perish but have eternal life. For God did not send his Son into the world to condemn the world, but to save the world through him. John 3:16-17

For more info, contact us at the address at inside front cover.

How can someone receive help at Teen Challenge?

Teen Challenge offers residential programs for adolescents and for adult men and women. In many of the programs, there is no upper age limit, so many who come are in their 20s, 30s, or older. The program usually lasts 12-18 months and offers intensive training in how to overcome addictions and other life-controlling problems and begin to live in a personal relationship with Jesus Christ.

One key requirement for all prospective students is that they must want to be in the Teen Challenge program.

There are more than 1,000 centers in 115 countries around the world. Two hundred of these are in the USA.

Please note that the admission requirements are not the same at each center. Most centers work only with men or women. Some work exclusively with adolescents.

For additional information on entering the Teen Challenge program, contact a center near you.

USA listing: www.TeenChallengeUSA.com

International listing: www.GlobalTC.org

How Teen Challenge is supported

Teen Challenge provides ministry programs to youth, adults and families who are faced with addictions and crises. We also offer a variety of prevention related programs and resources for use in local churches, public schools and other community settings.

Teen Challenge is a non-profit charitable organization funded by friends of this ministry. All donations are tax-deductible.

One of the greatest needs we have are friends who will help to provide scholarships for young people coming to Teen Challenge who have no financial means of paying for the cost of the program. If you would like to sponsor a student, please call or write for additional details.

If you would like to make a donation to a Teen Challenge center, you can locate the address or website of that center at one of these websites.

USA listing: www.TeenChallengeUSA.com

International listing: www.GlobalTC.org